# Contents

Braised Beef Brisket

2 tablespoons olive oil
1 beef brisket (3 to 4 pounds)
Salt and black pepper
1 large yellow onion, diced
5 cloves garlic, minced
2 pounds Yukon Gold potatoes, cut into cubes
1 pound parsnips, cut into ¼-inch slices
1 pound carrots, cut into ¼-inch slices
1 cup dry red wine
1 cup beef broth
¼ cup tomato paste
1 teaspoon dried thyme
1 teaspoon dried rosemary
2 whole bay leaves

1. Heat oil in large skillet over medium heat. Season brisket with salt and pepper. Add brisket, onion and garlic; cook brisket 2 to 3 minutes per side or until browned. Remove to **CROCK-POT®** slow cooker.

2. Add potatoes, parsnips, carrots, wine, broth, tomato paste, thyme, rosemary and bay leaves to **CROCK-POT®** slow cooker; stir well to combine. Cover; cook on LOW 5½ to 7½ hours or on HIGH 3½ to 5½ hours. Remove and discard bay leaves. Slice brisket and serve with vegetables.

Makes 6 servings

 # Slow Cooker Classics

Roast Tomato-Basil Soup

   2 cans (28 ounces each) whole tomatoes, drained with 3 cups liquid reserved

2½ tablespoons packed dark brown sugar

   1 medium onion, finely chopped

   3 cups chicken broth

   3 tablespoons tomato paste

   ¼ teaspoon ground allspice

   1 can (5 ounces) evaporated milk

   ¼ cup shredded fresh basil (about 10 large leaves)

      Salt and black pepper

1. Preheat oven to 450°F. Line baking sheet with foil; spray with nonstick cooking spray. Arrange tomatoes on foil in single layer. Sprinkle with brown sugar; top with onion. Bake 25 minutes or until tomatoes look dry and light brown. Let tomatoes cool slightly; finely chop.

2. Place tomato mixture, 3 cups reserved liquid from tomatoes, broth, tomato paste and allspice in **CROCK-POT®** slow cooker; mix well. Cover; cook on LOW 8 hours or on HIGH 4 hours.

3. Add evaporated milk and basil. Season with salt and pepper. Cook, uncovered, on HIGH 30 minutes or until heated through.

Makes 6 servings

Pantry Beef Stroganoff

- **1 pound cubed beef stew meat**
- **3 tablespoons all-purpose flour, divided**
- **1½ teaspoons dried thyme**
- **½ teaspoon black pepper**
- **2 tablespoons vegetable or olive oil, divided**
- **1 can (10¾ ounces) condensed cream of mushroom soup**
- **½ cup beef broth**
- **½ cup chopped onion**
- **¾ cup sour cream**
- **3 cups hot cooked egg noodles or fettuccini pasta**
- **Fresh minced parsley (optional)**

1. Place beef, 2 tablespoons flour, thyme and pepper in large resealable food storage bag; shake to coat meat with flour mixture. Heat 1 tablespoon oil in large skillet over medium heat. Add half of meat; cook and stir 4 to 5 minutes or until browned on all sides.

2. Coat inside of **CROCK-POT®** slow cooker with nonstick cooking spray. Add browned meat, soup and broth; mix well. Heat remaining 1 tablespoon oil in large skillet over medium heat. Add remaining half of meat and onion; cook and stir 4 to 5 minutes or until browned on all sides. Remove to **CROCK-POT®** slow cooker; mix well.

3. Cover; cook on LOW 6 to 7 hours or on HIGH 3 to 4 hours. Stir remaining 1 tablespoon flour into sour cream in medium bowl. Whisk in ¼ cup of liquid from **CROCK-POT®** slow cooker. Return mixture to **CROCK-POT®** slow cooker; mix well. Cover; cook on HIGH 10 minutes or until sauce is thickened. Serve over noodles. Garnish with parsley.

Makes 4 servings

Chicken and Mushroom Fettuccini Alfredo

- 1½ pounds boneless, skinless chicken breasts, cut into 1-inch strips
- 2 packages (8 ounces each) cremini mushrooms, cut into thirds
- ½ teaspoon salt
- ¼ teaspoon black pepper
- ¼ teaspoon garlic powder
- 2 packages (8 ounces each) cream cheese, cut into pieces
- 1 cup (2 sticks) butter, cut into pieces
- 1½ cups grated Parmesan cheese, plus additional for garnish
- 1½ cups milk
- 1 package (1 pound) uncooked fettuccini
- Fresh minced basil (optional)

1. Coat inside of **CROCK-POT®** slow cooker with nonstick cooking spray. Arrange chicken in single layer in bottom of **CROCK-POT®** slow cooker. Top with mushrooms. Sprinkle salt, pepper and garlic powder over mushrooms.

2. Add cream cheese, butter, Parmesan cheese and milk to medium saucepan. Heat mixture over medium heat; whisk constantly until smooth and heated through. Pour over mushrooms, pushing down any that float to surface. Cover; cook on LOW 4 to 5 hours or on HIGH 2 to 2½ hours.

3. Cook fettuccini according to package directions. Drain. Add fettuccini to Alfredo sauce; toss gently to combine. Garnish with additional Parmesan cheese and basil.

Makes 6 to 8 servings

Mom's Tuna Casserole

- **2** cans (12 ounces each) solid albacore tuna, drained and flaked
- **3** cups diced celery
- **3** cups crushed potato chips, divided
- **6** hard-cooked eggs, chopped
- **1** can (10¾ ounces) condensed cream of mushroom soup, undiluted
- **1** can (10¾ ounces) condensed cream of celery soup, undiluted
- **1** cup mayonnaise
- **1** teaspoon dried tarragon
- **1** teaspoon black pepper

Combine tuna, celery, 2½ cups potato chips, eggs, soups, mayonnaise, tarragon and pepper in **CROCK-POT®** slow cooker; stir well. Cover; cook on LOW 5 to 8 hours. Sprinkle with remaining ½ cup potato chips before serving.

Makes 8 servings

Mediterranean Beef Stew with Olives and Sun-Dried Tomatoes

1½ pounds cubed beef stew meat

3 tablespoons all-purpose flour

2 teaspoons dried basil *or* oregano *or* 1 teaspoon each

½ teaspoon salt

1 tablespoon olive oil

1 can (28 ounces) diced tomatoes

½ cup beef broth

¾ cup halved pitted kalamata or black olives, rinsed and drained

¼ cup chopped sun-dried tomatoes, packed in oil

½ cup grated Parmesan cheese

Fresh sprigs thyme (optional)

1. Coat inside of **CROCK-POT®** slow cooker with nonstick cooking spray. Place beef, flour, basil and salt in large resealable food storage bag; shake to coat meat with flour mixture. Heat oil in large skillet over medium heat. Add meat in batches; cook and stir 5 to 6 minutes or until browned on all sides.

2. Add diced tomatoes and broth to **CROCK-POT®** slow cooker; mix well. Stir browned meat into tomato mixture. Cover; cook on LOW 7 to 8 hours or on HIGH 3 to 4 hours. Stir in olives and sun-dried tomatoes. Ladle into shallow bowls; top with cheese. Garnish with thyme.

Makes 5 servings

Slow Cooker Classics

Autumn Chicken

  1 can (14 ounces) whole artichoke hearts, drained

  1 can (14 ounces) whole mushrooms

12 boneless, skinless chicken breasts

  1 jar (6½ ounces) marinated artichoke hearts, undrained

 ¾ cup dry white wine

 ½ cup balsamic vinaigrette

    Hot cooked noodles

    Paprika (optional)

1. Spread whole artichokes over bottom of **CROCK-POT®** slow cooker. Top with half of mushrooms. Layer chicken over mushrooms. Add marinated artichoke hearts with liquid. Add remaining mushrooms. Pour in wine and vinaigrette.

2. Cover; cook on LOW 4 to 5 hours. Serve over noodles. Garnish with paprika.

Makes 12 servings

Hearty Chili Mac

- 1 **pound ground beef**
- 1 **can (about 14 ounces) diced tomatoes, drained**
- 1 **cup chopped onion**
- 1 **tablespoon chili powder**
- 1 **clove garlic, minced**
- ½ **teaspoon salt**
- ½ **teaspoon ground cumin**
- ½ **teaspoon dried oregano**
- ¼ **teaspoon red pepper flakes**
- ¼ **teaspoon black pepper**
- 2 **cups cooked elbow macaroni**

1. Brown beef 6 to 8 minutes in large skillet over medium-high heat, stirring to break up meat. Drain fat. Remove to **CROCK-POT®** slow cooker.

2. Add tomatoes, onion, chili powder, garlic, salt, cumin, oregano, red pepper flakes and black pepper; mix well. Cover; cook on LOW 4 hours. Stir in macaroni. Cover; cook on LOW 1 hour.

Makes 4 servings

Slow Cooker Classics

BBQ Turkey Legs

6 turkey drumsticks

2 teaspoons salt

2 teaspoons black pepper

BBQ Sauce (recipe follows)

1. Prepare BBQ Sauce.

2. Season drumsticks with salt and pepper. Place in **CROCK-POT®** slow cooker. Add BBQ Sauce; turn drumsticks to coat evenly. Cover; cook on LOW 7 to 8 hours or on HIGH 3 to 4 hours.

Makes 6 servings

BBQ Sauce

½ cup white vinegar

½ cup ketchup

½ cup molasses

4 tablespoons Worcestershire sauce

1 tablespoon onion powder

1 tablespoon garlic powder

1 teaspoon hickory liquid smoke

⅛ teaspoon diced canned chipotle peppers in adobo sauce

Combine vinegar, ketchup, molasses, Worcestershire sauce, onion powder, garlic powder, liquid smoke and chipotle peppers; mix well.

Makes about 2 cups sauce

Slow Cooker Classics

Homestyle Mac 'n' Cheese

12 ounces uncooked elbow macaroni (about 3 cups)

4 cups (16 ounces) shredded sharp Cheddar cheese

4 tablespoons unsalted butter, melted

2 cans (12 ounces each) evaporated milk

2 eggs, lightly beaten

1 cup milk

⅓ cup all-purpose flour

1 teaspoon dry mustard

½ teaspoon salt

¼ teaspoon black pepper

Toasted bread crumbs (optional)*

To toast bread crumbs, preheat oven to 300°F. Place bread crumbs on foil-lined baking sheet. Bake 3 to 5 minutes or until lightly browned.

1. Coat inside of **CROCK-POT®** slow cooker with nonstick cooking spray. Fill large saucepan with water; salt lightly. Bring to a boil over high heat. Add macaroni; cook according to package directions. Drain. Remove to **CROCK-POT®** slow cooker.

2. Add cheese, butter, evaporated milk, eggs, milk, flour, mustard, salt and pepper to **CROCK-POT®** slow cooker; stir until well combined. Cover; cook on LOW 3½ to 4 hours or until cheese is melted. Top with toasted bread crumbs, if desired.

Makes 6 to 8 servings

Slow Cooker Classics

Beef with Apples and Sweet Potatoes

2 pounds cubed beef stew meat

1 can (40 ounces) sweet potatoes, drained

2 small onions, sliced

2 medium apples, cored and sliced

½ cup beef broth

2 cloves garlic, minced

1 teaspoon salt

1 teaspoon dried thyme, divided

¾ teaspoon black pepper, divided

2 tablespoons cold water

1 tablespoon cornstarch

¼ teaspoon ground cinnamon

1. Place beef, sweet potatoes, onions, apples, broth, garlic, salt, ½ teaspoon thyme and ½ teaspoon pepper in **CROCK-POT®** slow cooker. Cover; cook on LOW 8 to 9 hours.

2. Remove beef, sweet potatoes, onions and apples to serving platter; cover with foil to keep warm. Let cooking liquid stand 5 minutes. Skim off fat and discard.

3. Stir water, cornstarch, remaining ½ teaspoon thyme, ¼ teaspoon pepper and cinnamon until smooth; whisk into cooking liquid. Turn **CROCK-POT®** slow cooker to HIGH. Cook, uncovered, on HIGH 15 minutes or until sauce is thickened. Serve sauce over beef, sweet potatoes, onions and apples.

Makes 8 servings

Cheesy Mashed Potato Casserole

- **4 pounds Yukon Gold potatoes, cut into 1-inch pieces**
- **2 cups chicken broth**
- **3 tablespoons unsalted butter, cut into small pieces**
- **½ cup warm milk**
- **⅓ cup sour cream**
- **2 cups (8 ounces) shredded sharp Cheddar cheese, plus additional for garnish**
- **½ teaspoon salt**
- **¼ teaspoon black pepper**
- **Minced fresh parsley (optional)**

1. Coat inside of **CROCK-POT®** slow cooker with nonstick cooking spray. Add potatoes and broth; top with butter. Cover; cook on LOW 4½ to 5 hours or until potatoes are tender.

2. Mash potatoes with potato masher; stir in milk, sour cream, cheese, salt and pepper until cheese is melted. Garnish with additional cheese and parsley.

Makes 10 to 12 servings

Slow Cooker Classics

Zesty Chicken and Rice Supper

2 boneless, skinless chicken breasts, cut into 1-inch pieces

2 large green bell peppers, chopped

1 small onion, chopped

1 can (about 28 ounces) diced tomatoes

1 cup uncooked converted long grain rice

1 cup water

1 package (about 1 ounce) taco seasoning

1 teaspoon salt

1 teaspoon black pepper

1 teaspoon ground red pepper

Shredded Cheddar cheese (optional)

Place chicken, bell peppers, onion, tomatoes, rice, water, taco seasoning, salt, black pepper and ground red pepper in **CROCK-POT®** slow cooker; stir well to combine. Cover; cook on LOW 6 to 8 hours or on HIGH 3 to 4 hours. Garnish with cheese.

Makes 3 to 4 servings

Slow Cooker Classics

Heavenly Harvest Pork Roast

- ¼ **cup pomegranate juice**
- ¼ **cup sugar**
- 1 **tablespoon salt**
- 1 **tablespoon garlic salt**
- 1 **tablespoon steak seasoning**
- 1 **teaspoon black pepper**
- 1 **pork roast, any type (4 to 5 pounds)**
- 2 **pears, cored, peeled and sliced thick**
- ½ **orange with peel, sliced thick**

1. Combine pomegranate juice and sugar in small saucepan; cook and stir over low heat 2 minutes until sugar is dissolved. Pour into **CROCK-POT**® slow cooker.

2. Blend salt, garlic salt, steak seasoning and pepper in small bowl. Rub mixture over roast. Place roast in **CROCK-POT**® slow cooker. Turn roast to coat with juice mixture.

3. Top roast with pear and orange slices. Cover; cook on HIGH 6 to 8 hours. Serve with juice and fruit slices.

Makes 6 to 8 servings